LITTLE RICHARD and PRICKLES

by Patricia M. Scarry

Illustrated by Cyndy Szekeres

COLLINS
LONDON AND GLASGOW

Other titles in this series:
LITTLE RICHARD
WAGGY AND HIS FRIENDS

Originally published in U.S.A. by American Heritage Press, a subsidiary of McGraw-Hill, Inc.

This edition first published 1971
Second impression 1972
Published by William Collins Sons & Co. Ltd.

Printed by C. Tinling & Co. Ltd.
London and Prescot.

ISBN 0 00 138151 2

PICKING UP

Little Richard could not find his toy train.

He had looked for it everywhere—in the toy box, under the bed, and even in the chest of drawers—but the little train was not to be found.

He called his mother to help him find it.

When she looked round the room she said, "Little Richard, your room is so untidy that I'm not surprised you can't find your train. It must be here somewhere. Tidy your room and you will find it."

Little Richard's chin began to wobble, and his nose turned very pink, the way it always did when he didn't want to do something.

"Do you mean I have to tidy my room now, while I'm looking for my train?" he asked, his voice all high and squeaky.

"Yes, now," said Mother Rabbit. "Your toys are all over the floor."

“I’ll help you, Little Richard,” said a cheery voice at the door. And there was Prickles the porcupine, who had come over to play.

“Little Richard must tidy his room before he can play, Prickles,” said Mother. “Will you really help?”

“Oh, yes, Mrs. Rabbit,” said Prickles.

“That would be nice. Now I want to see a tidy room when I come back,” said Mother Rabbit as she left for the kitchen.

"I've lost my train, Prickles. I can't find it anywhere," said Little Richard.

"I'll help you find it, Little Richard. I'm a good picker-upper," said Prickles.

And he was, at first.

He picked up Little Richard's big green ball and bounced it around the room until it bounced right into the toy box.

He sailed a paper aeroplane until it landed in the toy box too.

Then he sat on the floor and piled blocks one above the other against the wall, until they were higher than he was.

"You're just playing, Prickles. You're not helping," said Little Richard, picking up crayons from the floor.

"Oh, I'm helping," said Prickles. "Just look how tidy the blocks are."

"But we've just got to find my train. It's my favourite," said Little Richard unhappily.

"Maybe it's in your bed. I'll help you look," said Prickles.

They both climbed onto the bed. And soon they were jumping on it, trying to see who could jump the highest, and squealing "Ooooh!" They almost fell off.

They crawled under the covers and pretended they were inside a tent. Then Prickles crawled off the bed and across the room with the blanket over him. The toys on the floor were dragged along by the blanket. And because Prickles couldn't see where he was going, he, and the toys, crawled through the cupboard door. He was funny to watch. Little Richard lay on the bed and laughed.

Inside the blanket it was dark. Prickles stood up, and there was a terrible CRASH! from inside the cupboard.

He had tripped on something and fallen down.

Then there was a squeal, and Prickles called, "I've found it, Little Richard! I fell over it." He crawled out of the cupboard holding up Little Richard's favourite train.

Oh, Little Richard was so happy!

"Mummy, come quickly. Prickles found my train!" he called, holding it tightly.

Mother hurried to the bedroom door. She was happy to see the little train again. Then she smiled as she looked round the room, with the blocks piled against the wall and most of the toys dragged off the floor.

"Well, now the room looks tidy," she said. "But you didn't have to put the blanket away, too!"

When Mother had gone off to the kitchen, Little Richard and Prickles hurried to the cupboard, shook out the blanket and put it neatly back on the bed.

Of course all the toys fell onto the floor again. But Little Richard was happy. He had found his train. And they would tidy the room later.

NAUGHTY OWLEY

Owley was a good friend of Little Richard's and Prickles'. He was full of fun and mischief. He was mischievous because sometimes he did things that his mother told him not to do.

And that is how his Big Embarrassment happened.

One day Little Richard and Prickles were playing when they saw an amazing sight! They saw Owley staggering across the meadow with a huge china biscuit jar jammed down over his head. It rested on top of his beak!

Of course his two friends ran over and asked, "Why are you wearing that big biscuit jar, Owley?"

"It looks awfully funny," said Little Richard.

"Well, it doesn't feel very funny. I can't see a thing. And my mother's going to be really cross this time," groaned Owley. Then he sat himself down on the grass with a plunk.

"It won't come off," he said.
Little Richard and Prickles
both pulled at the jar,
but it was stuck on tightly.

And all they did was
drag the jar, with Owley in it,
a few inches across the grass.

“How did it happen?” asked Prickles.

“It was an accident,” explained Owley. “My mother told me I couldn’t have any biscuits today because I’d eaten them all yesterday. But I knew there was one last biscuit down at the bottom. And when I couldn’t reach it, I stuck my head into the jar, and . . . here I am!”

"Poor Owley. Now your mother will be very cross," said Prickles.

"Maybe we could break it with a stone," suggested Little Richard.

"No! No! It's made of good china. Don't break it, please!" begged Owley.

"Never mind. My mother will know how to get it off. Come along, Owley," said Little Richard.

The two friends helped poor Owley to his feet and took him to Little Richard's house.

When Mrs. Rabbit looked out she tried not to laugh. What a sight Owley was! But, of course, she didn't ask him how it had happened. She could see that!

She just said, "Owley will have to stand on his head. We'll oil it off."

She hurried into the kitchen and came out to the garden holding a jar of salad oil. Then she said, "Could you please turn Owley upside-down?"

Now that was a bit of a struggle for Little Richard and Prickles. They had to turn the biscuit jar so that it sat on the grass. Then they hung on to Owley, who was upside-down in the air.

“Wh—what’s happening?” asked Owley nervously from inside the jar.

“It won’t hurt a bit, dear. Just shut your eyes while I pour this oil around the rim of the jar,” said Mother Rabbit.

“Eeeeeh! It feels horrible!” groaned Owley.

“It looks worse,” giggled Prickles.

When Mother Rabbit had oiled the rim of the jar, she rubbed it with her paw. Then she held on to the jar while Owley’s friends held on to him, and everyone at once shouted, “Pull!”

Pop! Out of the jar popped Owley.

Mother Rabbit wrapped a towel around his head to soak up the oil. And Owley sat up on the grass and smiled happily. He thanked Mrs. Rabbit and his friends very much.

Then Mother Rabbit washed out the beautiful biscuit jar so that not a drop of oil showed.

Owley dragged it home across the meadow, still wearing the towel on his head.

When he got home he told his mother everything that had happened. Then he promised to be good, forever.

Mrs. Owl was so happy to hear his promise that she hugged him and said, “But I love you just the way you are!”

POCKETS

Little Richard was wearing his very first suit.

It was a beautiful shade of blue, and it had many pockets.

"You look handsome in your new suit," said Mother Rabbit.

"And very grown-up," said Father.

"But everyone will stare at me. They will ask me what the pockets are for," said Little Richard, feeling shy.

"Tell them that pockets are to put things in," said Father Rabbit. And he dropped a shiny penny into the very top pocket.

Right away the suit didn't feel quite so new.

Little Richard put his paws in his side pockets and said, "Thank you, Daddy. I think I'll go for a walk."

The first friend he met was Prickles.

"Hello, Little Richard. I like your new suit. What are all the pockets for?" asked Prickles.

"They are to put things in," said Little Richard.

Prickles stared at Little Richard's new suit. Then he said, "You can have this pine cone to put in your pocket. I just found it."

It was a very big pine cone, and it took a bit of pushing, but at last it made a nice lump in Little Richard's pocket.

"Thank you, Prickles. Now my suit doesn't feel so new," said Little Richard.

“Let’s show your new suit to Owley,” said Prickles.

And off they went to his house. Owley said that the new suit was very nice. He especially liked the pockets. Then he offered his friends some fudge that his mother had just made.

“Take as much as you want,” he said.

Mmmm, it smelled warm and sticky. Little Richard took one piece for eating and stuffed two other pieces in his pocket.

Then they wandered down to the stream where they met Raccoon, who was fishing. He admired Little Richard's new suit.

"We're trying to fill up his pockets," said Prickles.

Raccoon dug into his bucket and said, "Would you like this nice little fish to put in your pocket, Little Richard? It's dead."

And of course Little Richard was delighted to fill up his very last pocket.

Father Rabbit was working in the garden. And when he saw Little Richard with his pockets bulging, he laughed and laughed.

"Now your suit doesn't look so new, Little Richard," he said.

"That's because we filled up all the pockets," said Prickles. "I'll bet his mother will be surprised when she sees him!"

And she was.

OFF TO SEA!

Little Richard and Prickles were playing near the pond one day when they found a funny old table that someone had left propped against a tree.

It had short little stumps for legs and a rope tied round one leg.

"Now that's a nice piece of wood," said Prickles. "I wonder what we could do with it."

They both looked at the old table and thought and thought. Then Prickles said, "Little Richard, we could turn it upside-down and put it in the pond, and it would be a raft!"

"And we could sail it and pretend we were pirates," said Little Richard, very excited.

Oh, this would be fun—because neither of them had ever been on a raft before. They turned the table upside-down so that the legs sat up, and they dragged it to the pond.

"Pirates always have flags on their ships," said Little Richard.

So they made one. They found a long stick and tied Prickles's sweater to it. Then they pushed the table out onto the water and jumped aboard.

It was exciting to float on the pond, although the raft did tip and lurch a bit.

"Hello, Mrs. Duck. We're being pirates!" called Little Richard, waving his flag.

“That’s very nice, dear. But I hope that you and Prickles know how to swim,” quacked Mrs. Duck.

“Oh, we’re not going into the water, Mrs. Duck. We’re just going to float on it,” called Prickles. And he paddled the raft along with his paw. They got it going nicely so that they were almost across the pond and near the stream.

Suddenly Little Richard felt a bit damp and chilly where he was kneeling in the raft. Oh, his trousers were getting wet!

Prickles stood up and said, "Little Richard, we've got a leak in our raft. Water is coming in."

Oh, dear. They knew it was dangerous to have water inside a boat. It was supposed to be outside. They tried scooping up the water and splashing it into the pond. But the water was coming in fast.

Because they were so busy trying to keep their raft afloat, they didn't notice that it had floated into the stream. And now they were being carried down the swiftly moving stream, with the water inside the raft growing deeper.

"Oooh, Little Richard, our raft is sinking!" Prickles wailed.

The two pirates were now quite frightened because the stream was swift and deep. And they didn't know how to stop their raft.

Suddenly Raccoon appeared on the bank of the stream.

The pirates called to him, "Help! We're sinking!"

Raccoon ran alongside the raft and shouted, "Throw me a line."

"A line?" asked Prickles, patting his pockets. "What is a line?"

"The rope that's tied to the table leg, that's a line," said Little Richard. He reached for it and flung it just as hard as he could. It sailed through the air, and Raccoon caught it. What good luck!

Raccoon pulled on the rope. Then he wound it around a rock and pulled the pirates' raft to shore.

Prickles and Little Richard were very happy to be on dry land again. They thanked their friend very much for saving them. Then they sat on the bank of the stream and chatted.

"I still think that table is good for something," said Prickles.

They all thought and thought.

It was Raccoon who had the best idea.

They pulled the table ashore. They worked hard for a while. And then they were very pleased with themselves.

They had found four big stones and had perched the table legs on top of them. With the flag planted outside, it made a wonderful fort! They played in it all afternoon.

BABY-SITTING

"Your babies are crying, Mrs. Hedgehog," said Little Richard.

"They've climbed out of their cradle," said Prickles.

"Yes, they're crying because it's naptime," sighed Mrs. Hedgehog. She pulled a dry sock off the clothesline and called to her babies, "Climb into your cradle, dears. Mother will rock you to sleep."

Prickles and Little Richard chased the babies and helped to put them into their cradle.

"They just won't sleep unless they're rocked," said Mother Hedgehog. "And they must nap before we go to the store."

Prickles and Little Richard helped to rock the cradle, and right away the babies stopped crying.

"Why don't you go to the store now, Mrs. Hedgehog? Prickles and I will baby-sit for you," said Little Richard.

"Oh, my goodness, that would be wonderful!" said Mrs. Hedgehog. She picked up her shopping bag and hurried down the lane. Then she looked back at her babies rocking quietly in their cradle.

"Good-by, darlings!" she called. Of course the little hedgehogs sat up.

"Now, go to sleep," said Little Richard, pushing at the cradle.

Prickles pushed too, and soon the cradle was rocking wildly. The little hedgehogs loved it.

"Your mother promised you'd sleep if you were rocked," said Prickles.

The cradle was rocking dangerously now. Then, whoops! It turned right over, and the babies tumbled onto the grass. They ran behind the tree where the clothes-line hung and climbed into the laundry basket.

"Now they'll never take their nap," said Prickles.

"Yes, they will," said Little Richard. He climbed into the cradle and called, "Look at me. I'm going to sleep in your bed."

Soon the baby hedgehogs were scrambling into the cradle. They bounced on top of Little Richard.

CRACK!

The cradle broke in two.

“Oooooh!” the hedgehogs all began to cry at once when they saw their broken cradle.

Little Richard tried making funny faces, but he frightened them. The baby sitters were beginning to need a nap too.

"Maybe we could make a hammock out of a sheet to rock them in," said Prickles. He dug in the laundry basket. No sheets.

Then Little Richard looked at the clothesline and saw Mr. Hedgehog's overalls hanging there, stiffly dry and covered with pockets.

"Now *there* is a good cradle," he said, grinning. And it was.

Oh, how Mrs. Hedgehog laughed when she saw her baby sitters! They both sat under the tree pulling the legs of Mr. Hedgehog's overalls. Back and forth they rocked, and the pockets were filled with little hedgehogs—all fast asleep.

"What good baby sitters you are. Why, you can sit for me every day if you'd like to," said Mrs. Hedgehog happily.

"Thank you, Mrs. Hedgehog," called Prickles and Little Richard. They hurried down the lane; for the overalls had stopped rocking, and those busy babies were waking up again.

DRIP! DRIP! DRIP!

It was raining.

What to do on a rainy day?

Little Richard had gone to Prickles's house, where they played all the games they could think of. Then they went outdoors and hopped from puddle to puddle all the way to Little Richard's house.

They sailed boats in the bathtub for a while. Then they decided to visit Owley and see what he was doing.

Poor Owley. He had been naughty again, you could just tell. When he opened the front door, he was holding a big wet mop.

"Hello, Owley. What are you doing?" asked Little Richard.

"I'm scrubbing all the stairs," said Owley.

"Why? What happened?" asked Prickles.

"Oh, it was an accident," explained Owley. "This morning I took a big pot of honey and some bread and sat on the top stair, and the honey pot spilled. It just ran away, all the way down the stairs." He sighed heavily.

"And now you have to clean it up!" said Little Richard.

"We'll be glad to help, if your mother won't mind," said Prickles.

"Mother is out shopping. And she didn't say I couldn't have company. She just said I had to scrub the stairs," said Owley. With a big smile, he opened the door wide, and his friends hurried in out of the rain.

“Oh, look at all those sticky stairs!” said Little Richard.

“But it won’t take long with three of us working. Let’s start at the bottom and work up,” said Prickles.

Soon the three friends were soaping and scrubbing and chatting as they worked their way up to the attic. At least it was something to do on a rainy day.

At last they reached the very top stair. It was Prickles who got there first. And when he saw Owley's attic, he let out a whoop! "Oooh! Look at all those funny things!"

Little Richard climbed over the top step and smiled as he looked round the big attic.

And Owley said, "Those are just old-fashioned clothes and things. We've got trunks and trunks filled with them."

There were funny, old-fashioned hats, and beads, and feather shawls. And even an old baby's pram with a parasol on the top.

"Now *this* is the place for a rainy day!" said Prickles.

Owley was pleased, because now that his punishment was over, he could play with his friends.

When Mrs. Owl came home, she was delighted to see the stairs all scrubbed and clean. She called, "Whoo! Whoo! Owley, where are you? The stairs look lovely, dear!"

She climbed up the stairs, looking for her Owley.

When she reached the attic she stopped. Then she laughed and laughed. For Little Richard and Prickles and Owley were all dressed up in old-fashioned clothes. And in the old baby's pram sat Owley, while Prickles and Little Richard pushed him about!

"May we go outside like this, Mother, please?" begged Owley.

And Mrs. Owl said,
why, of course they could.
So they carried the pram
down those long, long stairs.
And they pushed the pram down the lane with Owley in it. They felt so elegant and grand in those fine old clothes that they didn't mind the raindrops at all. And everyone ran outdoors to see them!

FISHERMAN'S LUCK

Little Richard and Prickles were going fishing.

They had spent the morning making new fishing rods. And Mrs. Rabbit had given them a big bucket to carry all the fish home in.

"Good luck!" she called from the door.

"Thank you, Mummy. We'll bring home a big, big fish for supper," said Little Richard.

"Big enough for all of us," called Prickles.

And off they went to the stream, with high hopes.

They settled themselves under a big tree, and they could hardly wait to use their new fishing rods.

Little Richard picked up his rod and swung it towards the water. Up, up went the string. But the hook landed in the grass.

"You have to swing the rod higher to make the hook land in the stream," said Prickles.

So Little Richard tried again. He swung his rod so hard that the hook sailed way out into the stream and caught on an old stump that was floating by. Oh, dear!

Little Richard pulled hard, trying to free his line from

the log. But the log kept on floating downstream, pulling Little Richard and his fishing rod behind it. Little Richard ran on the grass to keep up with the log.

"Let go, Little Richard. Let go of the fishing rod," called Prickles. For that log had caught the fishing rod and was determined to keep it.

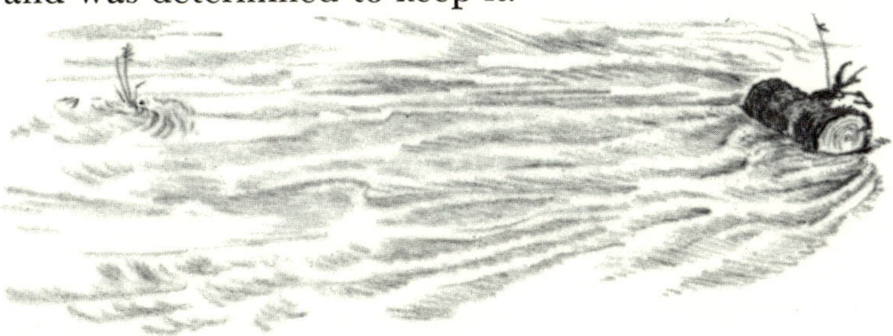

Poor Little Richard. At last he let go and glumly marched back to Prickles. He flung himself on the grass and pulled a sad face about losing that new rod he'd made.

"And we won't bring home a big fish for supper, either," he said.

"Oh, yes, we will. We'll catch the fish on my line. We'll take turns throwing it, Little Richard," said Prickles.

"Thank you, Prickles. It's your turn now. Throw it far, far out into the middle of the stream," said Little Richard.

Prickles held his fishing rod firmly. And he gave a huge jump as he swung the line towards the stream.

But—what happened?

Prickles had jumped so high that the fishing line flew into the air and wrapped itself round a branch in the tree overhead! Prickles found himself dangling at the end of his fishing rod.

"Little Richard, I have to climb into this tree and save my fishing rod," wailed Prickles.

"Swing up!" called Little Richard, giving his friend a big push.

Prickles swung hard. And soon he'd pulled himself up into the tree, where he tried to untangle his fishing line.

Down below, Little Richard could hear Prickles muttering.

"It won't come loose, Little Richard. I'm going to have to leave it up here in the tree," called Prickles crossly.

"Now we've both lost our new fishing rods. And we won't have any fish for supper," said Little Richard, plunking himself on the grass.

But soon he heard some noises coming from up in the tree. Prickles was eating something and enjoying it.

Then Little Richard felt pips dropping down on him. Prickles called down, "Guess what, Little Richard? This is a cherry tree, and the cherries are delicious. I'm going to throw some down."

And he did.

Little Richard ate some. They were sweet and fat and juicy. He had a fine idea. He held out the bucket, and Prickles dropped cherries into it. And when the bucket was all filled with cherries, Prickles slid down the tree trunk, and together they carried the bucket home.

It was lucky that Mother Rabbit just happened to have a big bowl of cabbage soup on the stove.

"I was making it for tomorrow's supper. But we can have it tonight," she said.

"And for dessert we'll have cherries in sugar and cream!" said Father Rabbit.

It was a wonderful supper. Everyone agreed about that.

"Well, we went out fishing and brought home dessert!" said Little Richard.

And everybody laughed.

THE BIRTHDAY PRESENT

Father Rabbit owned a dreadful old pair of boots that he liked. And he always left them wherever he stepped out of them. Sometimes he even left them on the living-room carpet, all muddy and wet. Mother Rabbit was not fond of those boots.

One morning when Prickles came over to Little Richard's house, he tripped over one of those boots lying on the front lawn. He kicked it along for a while, because he was thinking hard.

"Little Richard, today is my mother's birthday. Can you think of a nice present I can give her?" he asked.

"Maybe we could make her something," said Little Richard. "What does she like the best?"

"She likes flowers. And she likes old things," said Prickles.

They both looked at Mother Rabbit's garden of pansies nodding in the sunshine.

"I know Mummy won't mind if we dig up a few flowers," said Little Richard.

"But what could we put them in?" asked Prickles. "We have to find something old, like an old tree stump. Or . . ." and Prickles smiled. "What about this old boot? We could plant the flowers in this boot!"

"Oh, I don't know. It may belong to my father," said Little Richard.

"That? Why he wouldn't wear anything like that! See how the toe curls up? And it has no laces. Nobody would wear that!" said Prickles.

"Maybe you're right," said Little Richard. "We'll plant some pansies in this old boot now. I'll get the trowel."

The two friends dug up some flowers and gently planted them in the old boot. They sprinkled them with water.

Then they tied a pink ribbon around the boot.

It certainly was an unusual present. They were very excited, and they ran straight over to Prickles's house to give it to his mother.

Father Rabbit came home and kicked off his shoes. He looked under the bed and on the living-room carpet. Then he hobbled out to the kitchen, with one boot on, and said, "Mother, have you seen one of my work boots lying around? It's missing."

"No, dear, I haven't," said Mother.

"Oh, now I remember. I kicked it off in the garden last night because I had a pebble in it," said Father Rabbit. And he clumped outside
to look for his other boot.

"Mummy! Daddy! Come quickly!" called Little Richard. "Mrs. Porcupine wants you to come and see the birthday present Prickles and I gave her. She loves it!"

Mother and Father Rabbit followed Little Richard to Prickles's house.

"Isn't that beautiful?" asked Mrs. Porcupine. She pointed to her kitchen windowsill, where Father Rabbit's old boot was sitting, filled with Mother Rabbit's pansies.

"Why, it's lovely," said Mother Rabbit, smiling.

Father Rabbit looked down at his one lonely boot and frowned. Then he looked up with a big grin and said, "It's a wonderful present, Mrs. Porcupine."

Then they all sat down at the garden table for a piece of birthday cake.

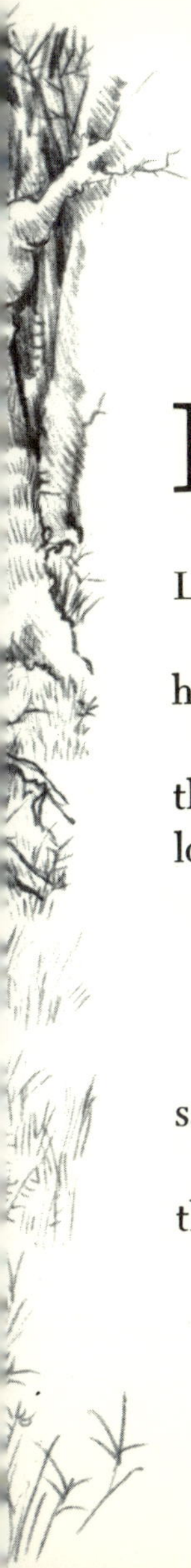

LOST

Little Richard and Prickles had been searching for chestnuts all afternoon.

"I must have seventy million chestnuts in my bag," said Little Richard.

"Me too," said Prickles. "Maybe we should start for home."

Little Richard and Prickles had been looking down at the grass for so long that they were surprised to see how low the sun had sunk. Soon it would be dark.

"Oh, we had better hurry home," said Little Richard.

"But which way *is* home?" asked Prickles.

"This way, I think," said Little Richard.

So they walked that way. But nothing looked quite the same.

"I remember that we passed some orange flowers, but they're gone," said Prickles.

“Flowers close their petals at bedtime,” said Little Richard. “But nothing looks the same to me. Let’s try going the other way.”

They turned round several times. And at last Prickles sighed and said, “Little Richard, I think we’re lost.”

The two friends sat down on the grass and watched the moon rise in the dark sky. They held paws for courage.

They heard the chirping of strange birds settling down to sleep in their nests and the rustle of small creatures in the grass. Every sound made the two friends jump with fright. So they tried to think of other things.

"Mummy will be setting the dinner table now," said Little Richard.

"I wish we were home. I'm co-cold." Prickles shivered.

Their shadows had grown long in the moonlight and frightened them when they looked behind.

Then suddenly, in the clearing ahead, a shadow came slowly towards them in the moonlight.

"What is that?" whispered the two friends, very frightened.

The shadow was growing longer as it came closer. Then two huge eyes stared out of the dark.

"Wh-who are you? A gh-ghost?" whispered Little Richard.

"Whoooo?" asked the shadow.

"Ooooh!" squealed Prickles.

Now the shadow seemed almost upon them. Two big wings flapped, and a familiar voice said, "Hello Little Richard and Prickles!"

"Is—is that you, Owley?" they asked.

"That's who!" answered Owley cheerfully.

Oh, how happy they were to see their dear friend.

"You gave us such a fright, Owley. All we could see was your shadow," said Little Richard.

"Well, I could see you very well because my eyes are better in the dark. Your mother sent me to look for you, Little Richard. Follow me. I'll take you home," he said.

Mother Rabbit was smiling at the front door. "I'm so happy to see you all. Thank you, Owley," she said.

It was wonderful to be home in the warm, bright house.

Owley stayed for supper. And so did Prickles. They laughed about their adventure.

Then for dessert Mother Rabbit served them steamed chestnuts, all soft and soaking in butter. *Mmmm*, they tasted good.

Both Little Richard and Prickles said it was almost worth getting lost just to find those chestnuts.

Well, almost!

FIRST SNOW

Little Richard ran from his room calling, "Mummy! Daddy! It snowed last night!"

Everyone hurried to the window to see the snow heaped like thick white icing on the meadows and trees. Then Little Richard hurried to get dressed. He hurried through breakfast. He hurried out into the snow and danced in it and flung it over himself. Then he began to make a big snowball.

"I'm going to make a snowman in my own garden," he said.

Prickles came running through the snow calling, "Little Richard, will you help me make a snowman?"

"If you'll help me make mine first," said Little Richard.

Raccoon came to help. He wanted a snowman in his garden too.

"I want a big, big snowman. As big as Daddy," said Little Richard.

Mother Rabbit called from the window, "Roll the snowball down the hill. It will gather snow on its way."

"But then it won't be in my own garden," said Little Richard.

"That's all right. You can see it from the window," said Mother.

So everybody pushed
at the big snowball. Slowly
it began to roll, faster and faster,
until it rolled away from them.
They had to chase it down into the meadow.
And they all laughed to see how fat it had grown.

Owley hurried from his house, very pleased. Because now the snowball was almost under his tree.

They worked all day. And at last the huge snowman stood round and smiling at the bottom of the meadow. He wore an old hat, and buttons of coal, and a long carrot for a nose.

Father Rabbit came down the hill, and he said it was the handsomest snowman he had ever seen.

"Now all of you hurry to our house, because Mother has made cocoa and buns to warm you," he said.

They raced up the hill, looking back at the snowman.

"Daddy, aren't you coming too?" asked Little Richard.

But the wind blew his question away.

Inside Little Richard's house, mittens and wet caps dripped by the fire. They all sipped cocoa and talked about their snowman.

"I don't really care if he isn't in my own garden," said Little Richard. "After all, we made him together."

"And we can see him from our houses tonight," said Owley.

"But only if the moon shines brightly," said Raccoon.

They were just finishing the buns when a snowball hit the window.

"It's Daddy," said Little Richard. Then he called, "Oh, come and look! Hurry!"

Everyone hurried to the window. They gasped and said, "Oh, isn't he beautiful!"

For down in the meadow, Father Rabbit had planted a ring of tall candles in the snow. They gleamed all round the snowman so that he glistened in the dusk for everyone to see.

"Now we can all see him from our houses tonight," whispered Raccoon.

"There's nothing quite like the first snow," said Owley.

And everybody sighed happily.